Five-Minute Bible Fun for Holidays

by Elizabeth Whitney Crisci

illustrated by Ron Wheeler

Cover by Jeff Van Kanegan

ISBN No. 0-86653-709-0

Printing No. 987654321

Shining Star Publications
A Division of Good Apple
1204 Buchanan St., Box 299
Carthage, IL 62321-0299

Unless otherwise indicated, the New International Version of the Bible was used in preparing the activities in this book.

Dedication

This book is dedicated to all the hardworking, unpaid, faithful pastors' wives (especially the ones I know personally) who serve so beautifully with their husbands in local churches.

To Parents and Teachers

Learning can be fun. Learning should be fun. Learning is fun when the teacher works at it. These pages overflow with ideas that will take an ordinary lesson and make it fun to teach as well as fun to learn. Time involved is nil in some cases, just minutes in other cases. Peruse the book and find what will fit the class for which you are responsible.

The idea of *Five-Minute Bible Fun for Holidays* is to make instantly available to Sunday School teachers and youth workers special additions to their programs and manuals; to make the lessons fit into the seasons of the year, and to make the hours more interesting; to catch the attention of the class and ultimately lead students to enjoy Bible study, Christian fellowship and, most of all, the Lord Jesus, who is the object of our faith, the reason for our teaching and the hope of our lives.

Each suggestion includes a list of needed supplies, preparation time, class time, how to present the idea to the class, and how to integrate it into the rest of the class session.

God bless you and your class as together you search the Scriptures.

Table of Contents

Winter Holiday Ideas

Springtime Holiday Ideas

Summer Holiday Ideas

Autumn Holiday Ideas

Winter Holiday Ideas

Resolutions

Time involved: Five minutes

Supplies: Pens or pencils, copies of acrostic

How-to for RESOLUTIONS:

Give each student a paper with the letters of RESOLUTION listed vertically on the left side for an acrostic.

R
E
S
O
L
U
T
I
O
N

Give the class five minutes to write one worthwhile resolution for each letter listed. Then have students share their resolutions.

Class integration: Let the list of resolutions introduce the lesson and show the need of living for Christ, knowing Christ, and letting the Holy Spirit guide us in our actions.

Plan Ahead

Time involved: Four to five minutes

Supplies: Pencils, paper, a large envelope

How-to for PLAN AHEAD:

Explain to students that resolutions are really goals. Some are attainable and some are not. If we don't have goals, we won't progress. Ask students to think of what they would like to accomplish this year: in school, at home, in church, and in their own personal lives. Give them a minute to think. Then hand out paper and pencils. Have students write down their resolutions and place them in the envelope. Ask one person to seal it. Put it away. In a few weeks or months, bring the envelope to class. Discuss students' goals. Give students their goal sheets and ask them how they're doing. Encourage them to keep trying to reach their goals.

Class integration: Discuss with students how God wants us to grow. By putting our goals into words, we can pray more realistically and remember what we want to accomplish for the Lord. Pray with the class about the fulfillment of their goals.

At the Stroke of Midnight

Time involved: Four to five minutes

Supplies: Timer, list of statements; scrap paper; pencil; small prizes: candy, cookies, bookmarks, calendars, pencils

How-to for AT THE STROKE OF MIDNIGHT:

Read a list of statements to the class. Students give themselves 50 points each time they can say "yes" to a statement. Let them keep their own scores. The object is to get 1000 points before the stroke of midnight (when the timer goes off). Set the timer for four minutes; then start the statements. Encourage students to be honest.

Suggested Statements (fifty points per "yes" response)

1. I brushed my teeth this morning.
2. I drank fruit juice at breakfast.
3. I have a dollar in my wallet.
4. I am wearing tie shoes.
5. I have more than one ring on my fingers.
6. I wear glasses.
7. I am wearing a sweater.
8. I am right-handed.
9. I read my Bible this morning.
10. I walked to class.
11. I brought my Bible.
12. I am wearing a watch.
13. I invited someone to come with me today.
14. I am going to try to please the Lord in the new year.
15. I have accepted Jesus as my Savior.
16. I plan to be in church each week this year.
17. I did my homework yesterday.
18. I helped my parents yesterday.
19. I want to treat adults with respect in the new year.
20. I memorized a Bible verse this week.
21. I will try to pay attention in the church service.
22. I participate in sports at school.
23. I say "no" to drugs and alcohol.
24. I love Jesus.
25. I smile often.

When the timer goes off, yell "Happy New Year" and ask each student with at least 1000 points to stand. Give each a prize.

Class integration: Remind students of some of the things they want to do in the new year. Pray for victory in their efforts.

Pass the Ball

Time involved: Five to six minutes

Supplies: A foam ball

How-to for PASS THE BALL:

Seat the students in a circle. As music is played (piano or a tape), students begin passing the ball around the circle to the left (no throwing allowed). When the music stops, whoever has the ball must tell a good New Year's resolution. Then that student starts the ball again, and it is passed until the music stops. Keep the game going for about five minutes. If a student is "caught" more than twice, the student to the left must then give the resolution.

UH... I RESOLVE... UH.. TO...UH... NOT SAY "UH" ANYMORE.

Class integration: Resolutions can really be prayer requests for better actions in our lives. Have students think about the resolutions that were mentioned; then ask God to help them start living them out.

God's Love

Time involved: Three minutes

Supplies: Paper and pencil for each student

How-to for GOD'S LOVE:

Discuss the importance of equality because God loves us all. Hand out pencils and paper. At the count of three, have students write down the different peoples that God loves. Suggest that there are more than just red and yellow, black and white. There are nationalities too. After two minutes, ring a bell. Ask students to count their answers. Let the student with the most answers read his list. Others may add to it. Repeat John 3:16 together.

Class integration: The topic of God's love fits into any Bible lesson. If the lesson is on salvation, talk about how God sent Jesus to the whole world; if the lesson is on Christian living, discuss the need to do away with "holier than thou" attitudes; if the lesson is on prayer, talk about the need to pray for more love between all peoples.

King for a Moment

Time involved: Three to nine minutes, as teacher desires

How-to for KING FOR A MOMENT:

Seat students in a circle. Walk around the outside of the circle, touching each student (lightly) on the head and saying "Martin," "Martin," "Martin." (similar to the game of Duck, Duck, Goose). As you touch one student's head, say "Martin Luther King." That student must stand up and explain a way to show love to someone, such as invite someone new to a party, bring a new student to class, sit beside a new student during assembly. If the idea is a good one, that student becomes IT and goes around the circle touching heads, saying "Martin, Martin, Martin Luther King."

Class integration: At the end of the game, pause for prayer. Ask God to help students show love to others, because He loves everyone.

King Matchups

Time involved: Four minutes

Supplies: Copies of matchups, pencils

How-to for KING MATCHUPS:

At the count of three, students should draw a line to match up each word on the right with a word or name on the left. Each answer has something to do with the civil rights movement or prominent black people.

Matchups

1. King's wife	a. Great Emancipator
2. Sammy Davis	b. Black
3. Lincoln	c. opera singer
4. Ethiopian	d. King
5. Martin Luther	e. Coretta
6. African American	f. eunuch
7. Civil	g. Jr.
8. Marian Anderson	h. rights

Answers: 1. e, 2. g, 3. a, 4. f, 5. d, 6. b, 7. h, 8. c

The first student to finish may read the answers.

Class integration: Praise God for those of the black community that have made life better for everyone. Praise God for those of every race who have committed their lives to Jesus Christ and made a difference in the world.

Heart Puzzle

Time involved: Three minutes

Supplies: Paper, scissors, envelopes

How-to for HEART PUZZLE:

Before class copy the heart puzzle for each student. Cut each one apart as shown, and put the pieces of each puzzle in a separate envelope. Give each student a puzzle. See who can put it together the fastest.

Class integration: Explain that love is a puzzle to us until Jesus comes into our lives. Any Bible lesson can easily bring out a message of love.

Love Pictures

Time involved: Five minutes

Supplies: A 9" x 12" sheet of white or manila paper for each student, pencils, crayons

How-to for LOVE PICTURES:

Have students fold their papers in half. On the left side, have each student print "Love Each Other" (1 John 4:7) in decorative letters. On the right side, each student may draw a picture illustrating one way to love someone who is hard to love. Let students share papers and explain their pictures.

Class integration: Whatever the topic of the day, Christian love can be included in the lesson. Close with prayer for God's help in showing love to others.

Love Shoes

Time involved: Four to five minutes

Supplies: A pair of men's shoes

How-to for LOVE SHOES:

Explain to the class that the shoes you are holding are "love shoes." Anyone who puts them on must act out a way to show love to others. Put the shoes on and act out a way to show love, such as telling one of the students, "God loves you." Then take the shoes off and give them to a student who will put them on and act out another way to show love. Suggest that students act out ways to show love at home, school, church, and other places they may go. Let each student have a turn.

Class integration: Read or quote 1 John 3:18.

Numbered Word

Time involved: Five to six minutes

Supplies: Bible look-up list for each student, NIV Bibles

How-to for NUMBERED WORD:

Give each student a Bible look-up list, a pencil, and a Bible. Tell the class to look up each Bible verse, count to the chosen word, and write that word at the bottom of their papers. When all the words have been found, they will spell out a secret message. Talk about how we can obey this secret message.

2nd word in John 14:25

5th word in John 16:22

6th word in John 15:23

3rd word in John 13:34

Last word in John 15:10

6th word in John 15:12

23rd word in John 10:1

Answer: "This is my command: Love each other." (John 15:17)

Class integration: The message of love for each other fits in any lesson because it is God's message to each of us. Work it into the opening, the closing as a final challenge, or any place in the lesson to provide a fun but meaningful break.

Secret Valentines

Time involved: Five to six minutes

Supplies: $5^1/_2$" x $8^1/_2$" sheets of paper, small paintbrushes, several small cups of lemon juice, electric iron and ironing board, envelopes

How-to for SECRET VALENTINES:

Give each student a sheet of paper and a paintbrush. Place cups of lemon juice on the table to be shared by several students. Each student may write a secret valentine message to share with a loved one. You may need to help some students "write" with the paintbrushes dipped in lemon juice. The words will be invisible. When they finish, let students come to the ironing board and press their papers with the warm iron to make the writing appear. The teacher should iron the valentines for younger children. Students may place their valentines in envelopes to deliver them.

Class integration: Briefly discuss God's desire for us to express love to others. Pray that those who receive these valentines will know God's love.

God's Love Drill

Time involved: Three to four minutes

Supplies: A Bible for each student

How-to for GOD'S LOVE DRILL:

Have students close their Bibles and hold them above their heads. When you call out a Bible reference concerning God's love and say, "Love drill," students may try to find the verse. The first one to stand and, when called on, read the verse gets 1000 points. The second student gets 500 points. The student with the highest number of points after all the verses are read receives a small award–a bookmark, a piece of candy, or a pencil.

Suggested verses:

Psalm 146:8
Proverbs 15:9
Jeremiah 31:3
John 3:16
John 16:27
Romans 5:8
2 Corinthians 13:11
Ephesians 2:4
1 John 3:1
Jude 21

Class integration: Remind students that love is the most important thing in the world, and that "We love because He first loved us." (1 John 4:19). Ask volunteers to share how God has shown His love to them this week.

Creative Bookmarks

Time involved: Five minutes

Supplies: Manila paper, patterns for bookmarks, silhouette pictures of Washington or Lincoln, stickers of the Presidents, pens, stars, glue, scissors

How-to for CREATIVE BOOKMARKS:

Discuss with students the many fine Presidents of our nation who have given us examples of good leadership, faith in God, and dependence on the Bible. Let each student choose a silhouette of Washington or Lincoln, or a sticker of a President, to put at the top of the bookmark. Suggest some Bible verses which may be written on the bookmarks, such as Psalm 33:12. Encourage students to decorate their bookmarks creatively. They may take their bookmarks home, keep them in their Bibles, or give them to friends or family members.

Class integration: Leave five minutes at the end of class to make the bookmarks. Students think about the lesson and thank God for a free country that allows them to study the Bible. Pray for the President before they leave.

"If I Were President" List

Time involved: Five to six minutes

How-to for "IF I WERE PRESIDENT" LIST:

Ask students to think about what they would do if they were President of the country. Encourage them to include Christian ideals in their thinking. Go around the circle, sharing ideas. Each student states his/her own idea, as well as those of students who have already had a turn. For example: The teacher says, "If I were President, I would give credit to people for going to church." The student to the teacher's left repeats, "If I were President, I'd give credit to people for going to church; and (the student adds his/her own idea) I would find a way to get drugs off the streets." The next student must repeat the first two and add a new suggestion. Continue until every student has had a turn.

Class integration: During the lesson, talk about some things we can do to improve our nation. Even one Christian can make a difference.

Hide and Find

Time involved: Four to five minutes

Supplies: Small, wrapped candies with Bible verse papers attached

How-to for HIDE AND FIND:

Before class, print the following Bible verses on small slips of paper. Staple or tape the Bible verse papers to small pieces of wrapped candy. Hide them around the room. When students arrive, tell them to find the candy and be ready to read the verses to the class. Count to three, then let the hunt begin.

Suggested verses:

Psalm 1:3
Proverbs 13:6
Psalm 24:3, 4
Psalm 106:3
Hosea 10:12
Matthew 12:35
John 14:24
Romans 5:1
2 Corinthians 5:17
Philippians 1: 11

Class integration: Make your own list of Bible verses. Choose ones that will help students begin the new year by putting the Lord first in their lives. Talk about the verses and pray that students will be willing to live God's way.

Snowball Fight

Time involved: Five minutes

Supplies: Cotton balls, two plastic bowls, chalk, list of questions

How-to for SNOWBALL FIGHT:

Divide the class into two teams. Appoint a captain for each team and have students line up behind their captains. Pile "snowballs" (cotton balls) at the starting line (marked with chalk on the floor). Place two empty bowls (one for each team) about three feet in front of the starting line. The first student on each team picks up a "snowball," stands on the starting line and tries to throw the "snowball" into the bowl. Each player gets three tries. If successful, the student is asked a Bible question. If the question is answered correctly, that student gets 1000 points. If the "snowball" gets into the bowl but the question is not answered correctly, the team gets 500 points.

Use the following list of questions:

1. How many books are in the New Testament?
2. What is the first book of the New Testament?
3. In what books do we find the Lord's Prayer?
4. Name two of the Gospels.
5. Name one of Paul's letters.
6. What is the last book in the New Testament?
7. What book comes before Matthew?
8. Name one book (other than the Gospel) that John wrote.
9. What New Testament books have First and Second?
10. In what book do we find "for God so loved the world. . ."?
11. What book tells us the most about heaven?
12. In what book do we find, ". . . the greatest of these is love"?
13. Who wrote Acts?
14. Who wrote Revelation?
15. What book comes after Revelation?

Class integration: This fun activity is a review of the Bible and an opportunity for students to stretch and let off steam. After the activity, the teacher may tell students, "Now let's see what else God's Word has for us today."

Winter Snow Art Calendar

Time involved: Five to eight minutes

Supplies: A calendar for each student (many businesses give free ones at this time of year), colored markers, art paper, rubber cement or paste

How-to for WINTER SNOW ART CALENDAR:

Have each student print a key Bible verse from the lesson on a sheet of art paper. It should be large enough to cover the picture on the calendar. Glue the verse sheet over the calendar picture. Students may decorate the Bible verse with winter snow art. Encourage students to use their calendars throughout the year.

Class integration: Explain that each of us has the same amount of time in the new year. How we use our time is important. Pray for a profitable year for God in each student's life.

Springtime Holiday Ideas

Make a Song

Time involved: Six to seven minutes

Supplies: Chalkboard, chalk, paper and pencils

How-to for MAKE A SONG:

Help the class make up a song about St. Patrick; then sing it. Use a familiar tune, such as "The Farmer in the Dell," "London Bridge," or "Alleluia."

Example: (to the tune of "The Farmer in the Dell")

St. Patrick served the Lord,
St. Patrick served the Lord,
Hi ho, the time is now,
I will serve the Lord.

Encourage everyone to participate in suggesting words for the song. Sing the completed song two or three times. If possible, have the class sing their song for their parents.

Class integration: Write the words of the song on the chalkboard so students can copy them. End class by singing the song, then praying that God will use each student in a special way, as He did St. Patrick.

Used March '93

Hunt and Find

Time involved: Four to five minutes

Supplies: A copy of the puzzle for each student, pencils

How-to for HUNT AND FIND:

Hand out copies of the puzzle and pencils. Have students circle the words listed beside the puzzle.

IRISH
LOVE
MISSIONARY
SAINT
PATRICK
MARCH
SERVE

M	S	E	R	V	E	A
I	M	P	J	G	U	V
S	A	A	O	C	O	K
S	R	T	L	O	V	E
I	C	R	N	V	X	M
O	H	I	R	I	S	H
N	G	C	T	L	A	N
A	I	K	I	S	I	S
R	H	O	Q	S	N	R
Y	A	R	C	H	T	P

Class integration: After students complete the puzzle, talk about how St. Patrick loved the Lord and spread His Word into Ireland. Talk about how we too can spread God's Word among the people we know.

Answers

M	S	E	R	V	E	A
I	M	P	J	G	U	V
S	A	A	O	C	O	K
S	R	T	L	O	V	E
I	C	R	N	V	X	M
O	H	I	R	I	S	H
N	G	C	T	L	A	N
A	I	K	I	S	I	S
R	H	O	Q	S	N	R
Y	A	R	C	H	T	P

Decoder

Time involved: Four to five minutes

Supplies: A copy of the coded message for each student, pencils

How-to for DECODER:

Hand out the coded message. After three minutes, ask the students to put down their pencils. Let a volunteer read the decoded message.

Like St. Patrick, I'll do this.

Code: A = 1, B = 2, C = 3, etc.

9 - 12 - 12	12 - 9 - 22 - 5	6 - 15 - 18	8 - 9 - 13
_ ' _ _	_ _ _ _	_ _ _	_ _ _
23 - 8 - 15	4 - 9 - 5 - 4	6 - 15 - 18	13 - 5
_ _ _	_ _ _ _	_ _ _	_ _

Class integration: After students decode the message, have them sing the hymn from which the words are taken.

I'll live for Him who died for me,
How happy then my life shall be!
I'll live for Him who died for me,
My Savior and my God!

Three Choices

Time involved: Four minutes

Supplies: A copy of the multiple choice activity for each student, pencils

How-to for THREE CHOICES:

Hand out the Three Choices activity. Tell students to circle the correct ending to each statement. Go over the correct answers as students correct their own papers.

Three Choices

1. St. Patrick's birthday is celebrated on the
   a. first Monday of January b. twentieth of March c. seventeenth of March
2. St. Patrick was a
   a. bookkeeper b. missionary c. doctor
3. St. Patrick served in
   a. Jerusalem b. Ireland c. China
4. God loves
   a. all people the same b. Irish people the most c. American people the most
5. St. Patrick was born in
   a. 387 b. 1429 c. 1949
6. St. Patrick is buried in
   a. Washington, D.C. b. County Meath, Ireland c. South Africa
7. St. Patrick preached that salvation comes through
   a. snakes b. good works c. Jesus Christ
8. St. Patrick was a
   a. Christian b. Moslem c. Hindu

Answers: 1. c, 2. b, 3. b, 4. a, 5. a, 6. b, 7. c, 8. a

Class integration: Talk about St. Patrick and his message of salvation through Jesus Christ. He loved people and wanted them to trust in the Lord.

Hidden Words

Time involved: Five minutes

Supplies: Praise picture for each student, crayons

How-to for HIDDEN WORDS:

Give each student a copy of the picture. Tell students there are nine hidden words of PRAISE in the picture. They are to circle the hidden words, and color the picture. When finished, let each student share one PRAISE word with the class. Remind them that these words are not only for Palm Sunday, but can be used to praise God every day of the year. Display the finished pictures on the bulletin board.

Class integration: Remind students that God wants us to praise Him every day. Close the class with praise prayers by the students.

Add a Word

Time involved: Four to five minutes

How-to for ADD A WORD:

Explain that together the class will make up a sentence praising God. They will do so one word at a time! The teacher will say the first word, and each student will add one word when it is his turn. (Example: I – will – praise – God – for – spring – flowers.) When the sentence is completed, repeat it together. Then play Add a Word again. This time, students will do a better job because they understand where they are heading. Remind them that their words will make the Lord happy. He always wants our praise, not just on Palm Sunday.

Class integration: We often praise God using other people's words in hymns, Bible verses, and poems. Today students get to praise Him with their own words. Encourage them to make up statements of praise at home, too. End your class with this time of praise.

Cross Puzzle

Time involved: Four minutes

Supplies: Cross puzzle for each student, paper clips

How-to for CROSS PUZZLE:

Select a key Bible verse. Print it on a cross which you have drawn on a sheet of $8^1/_2$" x 11" paper. Copy it for each student. Cut it out as indicated. Paper clip the pieces of each puzzle separately. Hand out the puzzles and give students three minutes to put them together. The first student done reads the verse to the class.

Class integration: Discuss the importance of the verse on the cross. Ask students why the cross is the symbol of Christianity.

Why?

Time involved: Four minutes

Supplies: A copy of the quiz for each student

How-to for WHY?

Give each student a copy of the quiz. Ask him/her to think of answers to the questions and be ready to share them aloud. Call on students to give their answers. Discuss the answer to the last question, reading the Bible verses to make sure students understand.

1. Why did you get up this morning?
2. Why do you go to school?
3. Why are your eyes the color they are?
4. Why do you like sports?
5. Why is Jesus your friend?
6. Why is the Bible true?
7. Why did Jesus die on the cross? (John 3:16; Romans 5:8)

Class integration: During the Easter season, students are thinking about Jesus' death. They need to understand why He died. Close with a prayer of thanks that Jesus died so our sins could be forgiven.

Because

Time involved: Four to five minutes

Supplies: Music or tape of "Because He Lives"

How-to for BECAUSE:

Sing or play a tape of the Gospel song "Because He Lives." Ask each student to complete the phrase: "Because He lives, I can..." You may begin by saying, "Because He lives, I can teach Sunday School each week." The student to the teacher's left completes the phrase next, and so on, around the class. Then sing the chorus of the song once more.

Class integration: Ask students why Easter is the most important day of the year. Point out that the Resurrection of Jesus is what gives us eternal life.

Emmaus Walk

Time involved: Five to six minutes

Supplies: Sheet of questions for each student, chalk, answer papers, pencils

How-to for EMMAUS WALK:

Before class, mark a path on the floor around the room with chalk. Place the answers along the path in scrambled order on small slips of paper. Give students the questions and pencils. They may walk the path, find the answers, and write them beside the questions. Take time to go over the questions and answers together when everyone is done.

1. In whose tomb was Jesus buried? (Joseph of Arimathea)
2. On what day did Jesus rise from the dead? (the first day of the week)
3. What big word says Jesus was alive again? (Resurrection)
4. After Jesus arose, who saw Him first? (Mary Magdalene)
5. Which disciple saw Jesus first? (Peter)
6. Who said, "Mary"? (Jesus)
7. How long was Jesus in the tomb? (three days)
8. How many men walked with Jesus to Emmaus? (two)
9. What happened to the guards at the tomb? (They shook and became like dead men.)
10. Who said, "He is not here"? (an angel)

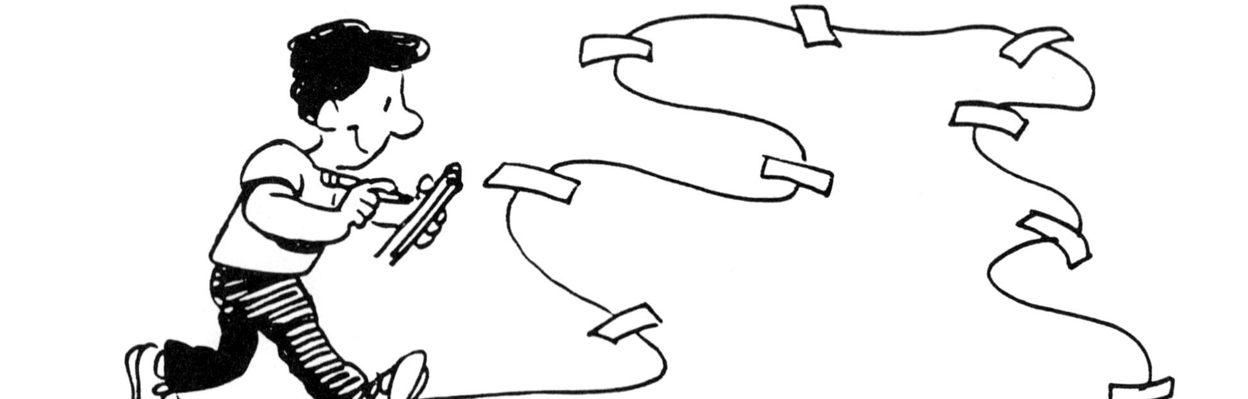

Class integration: Review the Easter lesson and reinforce the importance of the Resurrection with this fun activity.

Easter Verse Hunt

Time involved: Five minutes

Supplies: Ten empty tomb verse cards, Bible for each child

How-to for EASTER VERSE HUNT:

Print the following Scripture references on cards on which you have drawn empty tombs. Place them facedown on the table. Divide students into two teams and seat them on opposite sides of the table with their Bibles closed. Hold up a verse card. Students try to find the verse. The student who finds it first may read it aloud and gains 1000 team points.

Verses to use:

Luke 18:33	Acts 17:3
1 Thessalonians 4:16	Matthew 28:5
Mark 16:6	Luke 24:6
John 20:18	1 Corinthians 15:3, 4
Romans 6:4	John 11:25

Class integration: Discuss the verses students read. Ask students to tell why these verses are important.

Resurrection Helps

Time involved: Four to five minutes

Supplies: A copy of the Resurrection acrostic for each student, pencils

How-to for RESURRECTION HELPS:

Hand out the acrostic. Ask students to write a word beside each letter to describe an action or attitude that pleases our living Lord.

Suggested answers:

R = ready	R = ________________
E = enthusiastic	E = ________________
S = serving	S = ________________
U = useful	U = ________________
R = responsible	R = ________________
R = respectful	R = ________________
E = encouraging	E = ________________
C = caring	C = ________________
T = teachable	T = ________________
I = interested	I = ________________
O = orderly	O = ________________
N = nice	N = ________________

Class integration: Be sure students understand that when they receive Christ in their lives, He makes them new. They may make mistakes and sin sometimes, but they can confess their sins to God. He will forgive, forget, and help them to please Him.

Musical Bible

Time involved: Five minutes

Supplies: A Bible, a circle of chairs, Easter music to play on piano or taped music

How-to for MUSICAL BIBLE:

Seat students in a circle. As music is played, the Bible is passed from person to person. When the music stops, say a Scripture reference. The student holding the Bible looks up the verse and reads it aloud. If the student cannot find the verse, she may ask another student to help.

Verses to use:

John 11:25	Job 19:25	Matthew 12:40	Mark 10:34
Luke 18:33	Acts 2:32	Romans 6:9	1 Corinthians 6:14

Class integration: This is an interesting, fun way to have students look up verses related to the day's lesson. Choose your own verses to make the most out of this activity.

Promise Card

Time involved: Five minutes

Supplies: A 4" x 6" index card for each student, colored markers

How-to for PROMISE CARD:

Give each child a card and a marker. Have students print "My Promise Card to Mother" at the top of the cards. Then let them list five things they promise to do for their mothers, such as clear the table after dinner, help care for baby brother, speak kind words, hug you once a day, listen when you speak to me. Students may decorate their cards with pretty flowers and designs. Encourage students to give these cards to their mothers for Mother's Day.

Class integration: Explain that we need to show our love for Jesus by showing love at home. This card is one way each student can express love to Mother.

Hidden Mothers

Time involved: Four minutes

Supplies: List for each student, pencils

How-to for HIDDEN MOTHERS:

Give each student the list of Hidden Mothers and a pencil. The names are hidden in the groups of letters. The student should circle each name when he finds it. Share the answers.

Hidden Mothers

1. A S H A N N A H F O R K J (Hannah)
2. P O I U H G M A R Y Q W E (Mary)
3. Q S A R A H N J I O L K P (Sarah)
4. Q W R Y I P A N A O M I L (Naomi)
5. R E R E B E K A H M D M E (Rebekah)
6. Q Z E C T B U K O E V E S (Eve)
7. M A B E L R A C H E L P I (Rachel)
8. X J O C H E B E D O K E D (Jochebed)
9. B A R B A R A E U N I C E (Eunice)
10. W R Y I R U T H P K N F D (Ruth)

Class integration: Explain that God loves mothers and has given them the responsibility to train their children to love and serve Him. Praise God for parents.

Choose to Learn

Time involved: Five minutes

Supplies: Chalkboard and chalk or poster board and marker, a 3" x 5" card for each student, pens or pencils

How-to for CHOOSE TO LEARN:

Print three Bible verses about mothers on the poster board or on the chalkboard. Read the verses together. Ask each student to select one to memorize. Allow two or three minutes; then let students recite verses individually. (You may need to do some prompting.) They may copy their verses on 3" x 5" cards to keep in their Bibles.

Verse 1: "Honor your father and your mother, so that you may live long in the land the Lord your God is giving you." (Exodus 20:12)

Verse 2: "Listen, my son, to your father's instruction and do not forsake your mother's teaching." (Proverbs 1:8)

Verse 3: "A wise son brings joy to his father, but a foolish man despises his mother." (Proverbs 15:20)

Class integration: You may want to change the memory verse for today's lesson to use the Choose to Learn activity. Ask God to help students be more willing to listen to their parents and obey them.

Repeat and Add

Time involved: Five to six minutes

How-to for REPEAT AND ADD:

Call on a student to complete this statement: "I will obey my mother by. . . ." (The student may say, "going to bed on time.") Call on a second student to repeat the first student's statement and add a new phrase. ("I will obey my mother by going to bed on time and doing my homework.") The third student adds another phrase after repeating the two previous ones. Let every student have a turn.

I WILL OBEY MY MOTHER BY CLEANING MY ROOM.

Class integration: End the lesson by emphasizing that we need to please the Lord with our actions as well as our words. Do our actions at home please the Lord? Pause for silent prayer. Encourage students to confess their failures to show love in their actions at home and to ask God to help them.

5/9/93

Special Certificate

Time involved: Four to five minutes

Supplies: Pencils, papers, crayons or markers, large envelopes

How-to for SPECIAL CERTIFICATE:

Give each student a copy of the certificate and crayons or colored markers. Have children fill in the blanks. If a child does not have a mother, the name of grandmother, aunt, or other care giver may be used. Students may color the certificates and add decorations. Hand out envelopes. Students should address the envelopes, insert the certificates, and deliver them personally.

Certificate

"Honor your. . .mother" *Exodus 20:12*

This is to certify that

____

is the greatest mother in the world because

____

____

With all my love,

____

Class integration: Discuss with the class why it isn't easy to be a mother. Mother's Day is a great time to tell our mothers what a great job they do and how much we love them.

5/9/93

If

Time involved: Five to six minutes

Supplies: Circle of chairs, eight If cards

How-to for IF:

Sit with students in a circle. Begin spelling the word *mother*. Say only the first letter. The student on your left says the next letter, and so on, until the word is finished.

The student that ends the word must stand, take a card, read it, and complete the sentence.

1. If I were a mother and my child was caught swearing, I would...
2. If I were a mother and my child didn't come directly home from school, I would...
3. If I were a mother and my child made the wrong kinds of friends, I would...
4. If I were a mother and my child took something that didn't belong to him/her, I would...
5. If I were a mother and my child fought with a brother or sister, I would...
6. If I were a mother and my child was rude to an adult, I would...
7. If I were a mother and my child didn't do his/her homework, I would...
8. If I were a mother and my child went somewhere I had forbidden, I would...

After completing the If statement, the student begins spelling *mother* again, and the game goes on. If time permits, go through all the If cards.

Class integration: Remind students that it isn't easy to be a mother. They should obey and respect their mothers as God's representatives to train them in the right way.

Rock Tower

Time involved: Four to five minutes

Supplies: Stones, fine-tip markers, hot glue gun

How-to for ROCK TOWER:

Explain the word *epitaph*. Ask each student what message he would like to give others when he leaves Earth. Then using the stones and the hot glue gun, have each student build a rock tower. If time permits, children can use fine-tip permanent markers to print short epitaphs on their towers. Examples: God met my needs; Never forget God; Be happy; Give love.

Class integration: Some Bible lessons can lead to a discussion on death. Help students decide what important things they would like to accomplish in their lives here on Earth. Allow time for class discussion and sharing of the rock towers and epitaphs.

Why?

Time involved: Four to five minutes

Supplies: Eight Why? cards, circle of chairs

How-to for WHY?

Write questions on small cards. Some should be fun, some serious.

1. WHY must I go to school?
2. WHY is the ocean blue?
3. WHY do we have Memorial Day?
4. WHY do people die?
5. WHY do flowers bloom in the springtime?
6. WHY is ice cream cold?
7. WHY is the Bible true?
8. WHY did Jesus die?

Seat students in a circle. Stand in the middle of the circle, holding the cards. Point around the circle, stopping at one student. That student picks a card, reads and answers the Why question, and becomes "it." You may read the questions for younger students. The student who is "it" points a finger at another student. The same student should not be chosen twice until all have had a turn. Answers should be brief.

Class integration: A discussion of death near Memorial Day is important. Students need to realize that Jesus' death made ours just a stepping-stone to heaven.

Bible Memorial Days

Time involved: Four to five minutes

Supplies: A copy of the quiz for each student, pencils, cross stickers

How-to for BIBLE MEMORIAL DAYS:

Give each student a copy of the Bible Memorial Days quiz found below. Give students two minutes to answer as many of the questions as they can. Take turns discussing answers. Award those who have correct answers with cross-shaped stickers to remember Memorial Day.

Bible Memorial Days Quiz

1. Who died as the first murderer?
2. Name someone who never died.
3. Who died by his hair?
4. Who died by stones?
5. Who died by a slingshot?
6. Who died by hanging himself?
7. Who died by being beheaded?
8. Who died as the oldest man?
9. Who died before he could go into the Promised Land?
10. Who died between two thieves?

Answers: 1. Cain; 2. Enoch, Elijah; 3. Absalom; 4. Stephen; 5. Goliath; 6. Judas; 7. John the Baptist; 8. Methusalah; 9. Moses; 10. Jesus

Class integration: The Memorial Day celebration is a good time to explain the story of Jesus dying on the cross and being resurrected on the third day.

Family Tree

Time involved: Five minutes

Supplies: A copy of My Family Tree chart for each student, pens, crayons

How-to for FAMILY TREE:

Hand out copies of My Family Tree. Have students fill in as much information as they can. They may take it home and have their families help them fill it in. Talk about families. Ask students what they know or remember about family members who are no longer living, such as great-grandparents. Talk about how we may all live forever in heaven if we believe in Jesus.

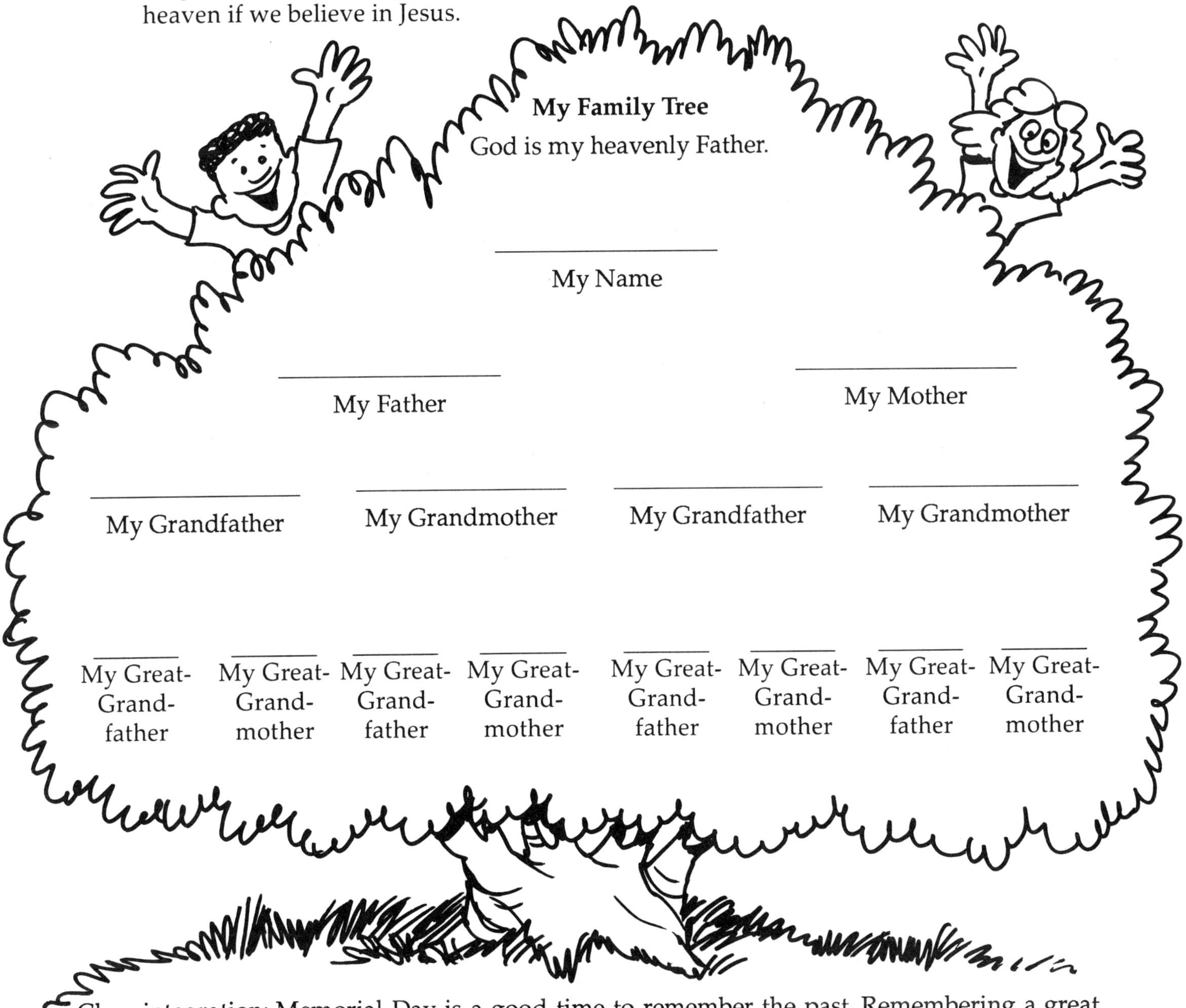

Class integration: Memorial Day is a good time to remember the past. Remembering a great family heritage will help each student see the world in God's perspective.

Flag Raise

Time involved: Seven to eight minutes

Supplies: A dowel or short flagpole (about three feet long), a national flag, thumbtacks

How-to for FLAG RAISE:

Talk about Flag Day as you hold up the flag without the pole. Announce that you are going to raise the flag together. Thumbtack the flag halfway down the pole. Every time someone says a Bible verse, the flag can be raised about an inch. Call on a volunteer to say a verse. If the verse is repeated correctly, ask the student to raise the flag to the next inch. Keep going until every student has said at least one verse and the flag is at the top of the pole. Place the flag for all to see and go on with the lesson.

Class integration: Ask a student to hold the flag during the closing prayer. Pray for the country, for peace, and for the salvation of its citizens.

Star Quiz

Time involved: Four to five minutes

Supplies: Paper flag, easel, gold stars

How-to for STAR QUIZ:

Before class make a large paper flag. Don't include any stars on the flag. In class, display the flag on an easel. Explain that students may "earn" stars to put on the flag by answering questions. After answering a question correctly, let the student put the designated number of stars on the blue field on the flag.

1. In what country did Moses grow up? (Egypt–two stars)
2. What place did God promise Moses? (the Promised Land–two stars)
3. In what city did Jesus grow up? (Nazareth–two stars)
4. What country did Columbus discover? (America–two stars)
5. In what country did Washington serve as President? (U.S.A.–two stars)
6. Who made the first American flag? (Betsy Ross–three stars)
7. In what country did Paul end up in prison? (Rome–three stars)
8. What country is north of the U.S.A.? (Canada–two stars)
9. What country is just south of Texas? (Mexico–two stars)
10. In what city did Solomon build the temple? (Jerusalem–three stars)
11. What country was the former home of the Pilgrims? (England–two stars)
12. How many original colonies were there? (13–four stars)
13. How many stars were on the first U.S.A. flag? (13–four stars)
14. In what town was Jesus born? (Bethlehem–three stars)
15. Where did Mary and Joseph go to escape from Herod? (Egypt–three stars)
16. Where was the Declaration of Independence signed? (Philadelphia–three stars)
17. What country did Napoleon come from? (France–two stars)
18. What three colors are in the American flag? (red, white and blue–two stars)
19. How many stars are on the U.S.A. flag now? (50–two stars)
20. What were the last two states to join the U.S.A.? (Hawaii and Alaska–two stars)

Class integration: Brainstorm reasons to praise God for our country (freedom to worship, enough food, etc.). Remind students that living in a free country makes it possible to study the Bible.

Sticker Fun

Time involved: Five minutes

Supplies: Flag stickers, construction paper, scrap paper, pencils

How-to for STICKER FUN:

Hand out construction paper, scrap paper, and pencils. Have students write praises to God on the scrap paper. When you clap your hands after two minutes, they must put their pencils down and count their praises. Have students read their praises aloud. Give each child one flag sticker for each praise he lists. Students may place the stickers on the construction paper and glue the praise lists on the back.

Class integration: Any Bible lesson is an appropriate time to praise God for the freedom to learn about Jesus and share Him with others.

What If I Were a Dad

Time involved: Four minutes

How-to for WHAT IF I WERE A DAD:

Discuss the difficulties of being a father. Dads love their children, yet they must discipline and train them. Have students think about how they would complete the sentence: "If I were a dad, I would. . . ." Suggest topics for students to consider: church attendance, making friends, discipline, schoolwork, free time. Let each student have a turn. Then discuss the responses.

Class integration: Use this activity to have fun and observe your students' desire to obey their parents. To allow for single-parent homes, you may want to change the wording to, "If I were a parent, I would. . . ."

5/23/93

Blue Ribbons

Time involved: Four to five minutes

Supplies: A $1\frac{1}{2}$" x 7" blue ribbon for each student, colored markers, small white circles or starburst shapes, stapler

How-to for BLUE RIBBONS:

Explain the significance of Father's Day: a time to remember and show love to our fathers. (For some it may be a grandfather, uncle, or stepfather.) Hand out blue ribbons. Have students print "First Prize" at the top of them. Print father's name on the circle or starburst; then staple it to the top of the ribbon. At the bottom each student should write who the ribbon is from. Encourage students to take the ribbons home and present them to their dads.

Class integration: End the lesson by reminding students that God has given us people to love and care for us. Father's Day is a time to say "thank you."

5/23/93

Dad's Gift

Time involved: Four to five minutes

Supplies: A sheet of 9" x 12" construction paper for each student, colored markers, glue, Scripture stickers

How-to for DAD'S GIFT:

Hand out construction paper, markers, glue, and stickers. Each student folds the paper in half, then in half again. When the paper is unfolded, there are four sections. On the third section down, the student writes a note to Dad (I love you) or about him (My dad is the best). A Scripture sticker may be placed on the same section. Have the student glue one of the end sections to the other to form a name plate for father's desk.

Class integration: Whether we have dads or not, we all have a heavenly Father who loves us more than any human being could. As you teach the lesson, refer to God as our heavenly Father and emphasize His love and care.

5/23/93

Another Dad's Card

Time involved: Four to five minutes

Supplies: A sheet of $8^1/_2$" x 11" paper for each student, colored markers, stickers, magazines, glue

How-to for ANOTHER DAD'S CARD:

Have each student think of a special man in her life, someone who is caring and helpful. Hand out paper, markers, stickers, magazines, and glue. Let each student create a special card for that special man. Print some suggestions on the chalkboard: "I think of you on Father's Day" or "You have been like a father to me" or "I love you like a father." Each student may draw pictures, use stickers, or cut pictures from magazines to make the card. Encourage them to give the cards to their special "dad for a day."

Class integration: Point out to students that many people help them grow up and learn how to live in their world. In a closing prayer, thank God for those special people He brings into our lives.

Find Me

Time involved: Five minutes

Supplies: A copy of the quiz for each student, pencils

How-to for FIND ME:

Hand out the quizzes and pencils. Ask each student to draw a line connecting each father and son pair. Note that some fathers have more than one son. Be sure to follow up by giving the correct answers and saying a short prayer to praise God for our own fathers.

Sons	**Fathers**
Joseph	Zechariah
Abel	David
Benjamin	Jacob
Absalom	Abraham
John the Baptist	Adam
Isaac	Zebedee
Cain	
James and John	
Solomon	

Answers: Joseph-Jacob; Abel-Adam; Benjamin-Jacob; Absalom-David; John the Baptist-Zechariah; Isaac-Abraham; Cain-Adam; James and John-Zebedee; Solomon-David

Class integration: The Bible is full of stories about fathers and sons. Share biblical father and son stories with students.

Gift Certificate

Time involved: Five minutes

Supplies: A sheet of 9" x 12" construction paper for each student, colored markers, glue, Scripture stickers

How-to for GIFT CERTIFICATE:

Talk about some of the things a father has to accomplish around the house. How could we make it easier for him? Let students suggest special jobs they could do to make life a little easier for their dads, such as taking out the garbage, loading the dishwasher, cutting the grass, or raking leaves. Let each student write a gift certificate for his father. (This is good for one hour of raking leaves.) Students may decorate the certificates and give them to their fathers on Father's Day.

Class integration: These gift certificates give students an opportunity to show their love by their actions. Make the idea of loving actions a part of the day's lesson.

Summer Holiday Ideas

SS2845

Salute

Time involved: Four minutes

How-to for SALUTE:

Seat students in a circle. Explain that when you salute a student, he must stand, salute back, and try to answer the question you ask. If the student's answer is correct, he remains standing and salutes another student. That student must stand and try to answer the teacher's next question. If a student cannot answer a question, he sits down and the one who gave the salute selects another student to salute. All who answer questions correctly remain standing until the end of the game. The standing students are the winners and should be given a round of applause.

Suggested Questions (For younger students, you may want to choose easier words.)

1. How do you spell B -I-B-L-E?
2. How do you spell O-B-E-Y?
3. How do you spell T-R-U-S-T?
4. How do you spell W-I-T-N-E-S-S?
5. How do you spell S-E-R-V-E?
6. How do you spell P-R-A-Y-E-R?
7. How do you spell L-O-V-E?
8. How do you spell H-E-L-P?
9. How do you spell G-I-V-E?
10. How do you spell C-O-N-F-E-S-S?
11. How do you spell F-O-R-G-I-V-E?
12. How do you spell D-E-D-I-C-A-T-E?

Class integration: This activity will help students think about God's Word and what it teaches about asking God for help. Emphasize that we can never live the Christian life in our own strength. First we need to receive Jesus as Savior; then we need to ask for strength through His Holy Spirit.

Firecracker Sentences

Time involved: Five minutes

Supplies: Paper with a large firecracker drawn on it for each student, pens, dictionary

How-to for FIRECRACKER SENTENCES:

Hand out the papers. Ask a student to read from the dictionary the definition of *freedom* or *independence.* Ask each student to write one sentence on "What freedom means to me." Answers may include "It means I can go to church, travel, vote for our country's leaders." Let younger students express their ideas verbally instead of writing them down. Ask students to share their ideas with the rest of the class.

Class integration: Explain that Jesus sets us free. If we love Him, we won't use our freedom to sin, but to serve Him.

Independence or Dependence

Time involved: Four to six minutes

Supplies: A quiz paper for each student, pencils, paper, stickers

How-to for INDEPENDENCE OR DEPENDENCE:

Read from a dictionary the difference between *independence* and *dependence*. Give each student a copy of the quiz. Give them three minutes to complete it. Then go over the answers. There are no right or wrong answers. Students may check one or both columns. Answers will vary according to the student.

Quiz

	Independent (I do it on my own.)	**Dependent** (Someone helps me.)
1. Schoolwork		
2. Living		
3. Setting Responsibilities		
4. Cleanliness		
5. Time Schedule		
6. Prayer		
7. Bible Study		
8. Dressing		
9. Eating		
10. Thinking		
11. Hobbies		
12. Church Attendance		

Class integration: None of us is completely independent. We need God, parents, friends, and others. Praise God for those who help us and for each area where we are learning to be more independent.

Bible March

Time involved: Five to seven minutes

Supplies: Flag, Bible memory verse printed on 6" x 8" paper, marching tape and recorder or piano, marching music and pianist

How-to for BIBLE MARCH:

Seat students in a circle, facing out. On one of the chairs place a sheet of paper on which you have printed a key Bible verse. Choose a leader to lead the class and carry the flag. When the leader starts to march, begin the music. When the leader raises the flag high, stop the music and have students sit down. Whoever sits on the chair where the verse has been placed reads the verse. That student may then put the verse on another chair, and the leader begins the march again. After three or four different students have read the verse, turn the paper upside down on a chair. The next student to sit on the verse must say it from memory. If the verse is repeated correctly, that student becomes the leader, and leads the march again.

Class integration: Choose a key verse for the day. Use the Bible March to help students learn the verse.

Hidden Shells

Time involved: Five to six minutes

Supplies: Seashells, Bible verses written on small slips of paper

How-to for HIDDEN SHELLS:

Before class, write on small slips of paper Bible verses important to the lesson. Roll them up and place them inside or under shells hidden around the room. Students may hunt for the shells, bring them back to the table, and remove the verses. For older students you may want to just put the Scripture references in the shells. Students may then look up the verses and have them ready to read aloud.

Class integration: Since this activity is built on Bible verses chosen from the day's lesson, it fits right in with the lesson aim. If possible, let students take some shells home.

5/30/92

Summer Bible Picnic

Time involved: Five to eight minutes

Supplies: A copy of the verses and a Bible for each student, pencils, punch, fruit sections

How-to for SUMMER BIBLE PICNIC:

Give each student a Bible and a list of Bible verses. Have students look up the verses to find the picnic food included in each. After four minutes, have students put their pencils down and read their lists. You may read the Bible verses aloud for younger students.

Bible References	Answers
Luke 4:4	bread
Genesis 49:12	milk
Galatians 5:22	fruit
John 21:8	fish
Numbers 11:5	fish, cucumbers, melons, leeks, onions, garlic
Isaiah 65:8	grape juice
Exodus 29:23	bread, cake
Psalm 78:20	meat

JESUS AND HIS DISCIPLES ATE FISH AT A COOKOUT!

Class integration: Have the class sit on the floor as if at a picnic. Serve punch and fruit sections. Use a picnic theme throughout the lesson. This activity will work well at the beginning or end of class.

6/30/93

Figure Me Out

Time involved: Four to five minutes

Supplies: A copy of the puzzle for each student, pencils

How-to for FIGURE ME OUT:

Hand out the puzzle and pencils. At the count of three, let students begin to work it out. Give them this clue: The answer is a statement that we sometimes sing, and it encourages us. The first student to figure out the answer receives 1000 points. Each succeeding finisher gets 50 points less. After three or four minutes, ask the winner to read the answer. Ask the runner-up to explain what it means.

Figure me out.

Clues: S = T C = A M = Y W = S O = E H = M D = V Z = R
L = D N = O K = N T = J A = U X = I Y = H R = F

M O W S O Z L C M, S N L C M, C K L

R N Z O D O Z, T O W A W X W S Y O W C H O.

Answer: "Yesterday, today, and forever, Jesus is the same."

Class integration: Choose a phrase or verse for this activity that relates to the day's lesson. Use this activity as a fun break in the lesson.

Baseball a la Bible

Time involved: Five minutes each week for several weeks or a whole class period one week

Supplies: Chairs arranged like a baseball diamond, game spinner

How-to for BASEBALL A LA BIBLE:

Before class make a game spinner by dividing a cardboard circle into five equal sections. Write on each section one of these categories: Base Hit, Double, Triple, Home Run, Out. Thumbtack a paper clip to the center of the circle for a spinner. Arrange four chairs in the classroom to look like a baseball diamond (three bases and home plate). Line up the rest of the chairs for the two teams. When students arrive, divide them into two teams. The first player spins to choose a category. Ask a question from that category. If it is answered correctly, the student sits on the appropriate "base." Players advance around the bases as usual. When a player reaches "home" the team scores one point. When a student gives an incorrect answer, the team receives one out. After three outs, the other team is "up to bat." Keep score on the chalkboard.

Single

Spell *Abraham.*
Spell *Psalm.*
Spell *Isaiah.*
Spell *Benjamin.*
Spell *Goliath.*
Spell *Saul.*
Spell *Moses.*
Spell *Genesis.*
Spell *Noah.*
Spell *Babel.*

Double

What book comes after
- Genesis? (Exodus)
- Exodus? (Leviticus)
- Leviticus? (Numbers)
- Numbers (Deuteronomy)
- Deuteronomy? (Joshua)
- Joshua? (Judges)
- Judges? (Ruth)
- Ruth? (1 Samuel)
- 2 Samuel? (1 Kings)
- 2 Kings? (1 Chronicles)

Triple

Who was the mother of Cain? (Eve)
Who was the sister of Moses? (Miriam)
Who was the father of Jacob? (Isaac)
Who was the brother of Abel? (Cain)
Who was the mother-in-law of Ruth? (Naomi)
Who was the father of Joseph? (Jacob)
Who was the father of Seth? (Adam)
Who was the twin of Jacob? (Esau)
Who was the father of Absalom? (David)
Who was the husband of Sarah? (Abraham)

Home Run

In what book do we find
- Mordecai? (Esther)
- the flood? (Genesis)
- the birth of Moses? (Exodus)
- Jesus' birth in Bethlehem predicted? (Micah)
- the Ten Commandments? (Exodus)
- the Creation story? (Genesis)
- Hannah's prayer for a baby? (1 Samuel)
- the lion's den? (Daniel)
- the parting of the Red Sea? (Exodus)
- Joseph's dreams? (Genesis)

Class integration: Discuss the importance of being familiar with the Bible. You may want to choose your own questions for the game from the day's lesson. For younger students, choose easier questions.

Labor Notes

Time involved: Five minutes

Supplies: A copy of the music puzzle for each student, pencils, scissors

How-to for LABOR NOTES:

Before class, make a copy of the puzzle for each student and cut it into eleven pieces (a word and note on each piece). Paper clip the pieces of puzzle together. In class, hand out the puzzles. Have students arrange the pieces correctly. If students line up the musical notes in a scale beginning with C, they will have the words in correct order.

Have students read the completed verse aloud several times; then have them turn over a couple of notes and read it again. Finally, have students turn over all the puzzle pieces and say the verse from memory.

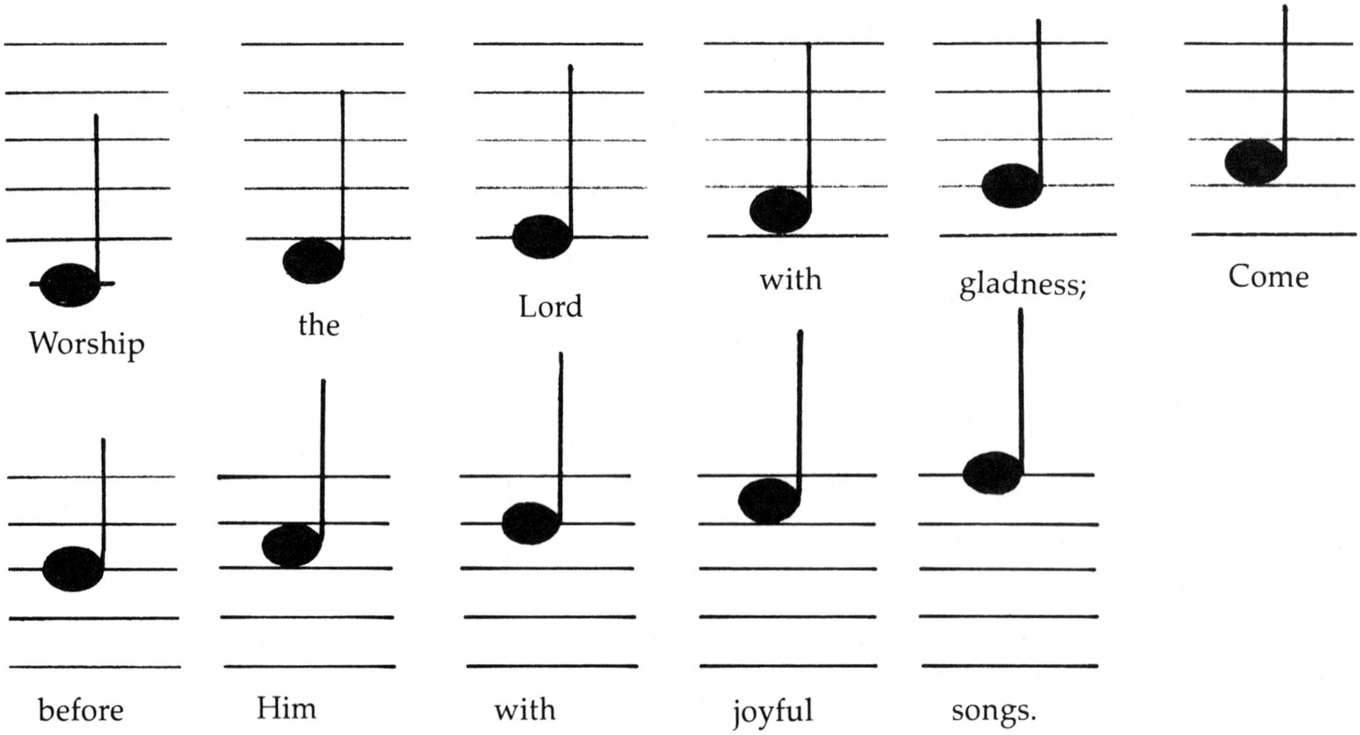
Worship
the
Lord
with
gladness;
Come
before
Him
with
joyful
songs.

Psalm 100:2

Class integration: As you talk about Labor Day, remind students that the only lasting labor is what we do for Jesus.

Lost Vowels

Time involved: Five minutes

Supplies: A copy of the incomplete verse for each student, vowels printed on small squares of paper hidden around the room.

How-to for LOST VOWELS:

Print the missing vowels on twenty-four small squares of paper and hide them around the room. Give each student a copy of the incomplete Bible verse. Have them hunt for the missing vowels and add them to the verse. Students may need to trade vowels with each other to get the ones they need. Choose a simple verse or message for younger students.

C___m___ t___ m___, ___ll y___ ___

wh___ ___r___ w___ ___ry ___nd b___rd___n___d,

___nd ___ w___ll g___v___ y___ ___ r___st.

Matthew 11:28

Class integration: Labor Day can be a reminder of the rest God offers us when we are burdened with sin. We can trust Him.

Bible Laborers

Time involved: Five minutes

Supplies: A copy of Bible Laborers for each student, pencils

How-to for BIBLE LABORERS:

Give each student a copy of the activity and a pencil. Allow three minutes for them to match the Bible workers with their jobs. Go over the answers together. Make this an oral activity for younger students.

Bible Person	Job
1. Cain	a. fisherman
2. Jesus	b. judge
3. David	c. doctor
4. Deborah	d. missionary
5. Luke	e. farmer
6. John the Baptist	f. carpenter
7. Peter	g. shepherd
8. Paul	h. preacher

Class integration: Explain to students that God wants us to do our best in any job we do. Ask them what they want to be when they grow up. Close with prayer asking God to show each student His will.

This Way to Work

Time involved: Four to six minutes

How-to for THIS WAY TO WORK:

Seat students in a circle. Sing the chorus together, changing the Bible character each time. The song is to the tune of "Here We Go 'Round the Mulberry Bush."

This is the way that Peter worked,

Peter worked, Peter worked,

This is the way that Peter worked,

In Bible days we read.

As the class sings, one student should act out the occcupation of the person being sung about (Peter–fisherman).

Other suggestions:

Cain–farmer

David–shepherd

Luke–doctor

Deborah–judge

Paul–missionary

Matthew–tax collector

Cornelius–soldier

Class integration: Talk about one occupation in the day's lesson. Emphasize the service to the Lord that was displayed.

Reading Class

Time involved: Four to five minutes

Supplies: NIV Bibles

How-to for READING CLASS:

Choose a Scripture passage for reading aloud. Some good ones are Psalm 23, Psalm 100, Matthew 5:3-10, and John 10:10-18. Divide the passage into three parts. Read each part a different way.

Part One: Read aloud as students follow along. When you pause, the class reads the next word in unison. Pause at key words of the passage. Students will catch on quickly and enjoy the reading. Pause often so they do not lose interest.

Part Two: Let a good reader read a verse; then the class may read the next in a responsive reading.

Part Three: Choose a student leader to lead the class as they read the verses in unison.

Class integration: Use this fun way to read a Scripture passage related to the lesson. Praise students for a job well done. Encourage them to live what they have read.

Library Time

Time involved: Five minutes

Supplies: A chart of Bible books or Bibles open to the index

How-to for LIBRARY TIME:

My best library is right here. (Hold up Bible.) It has sixty-six books. How many? (Let students repeat the answer.) There are thirty-nine books in the Old Testament. How many? (Students repeat the answer.) There are twenty-seven books in the New Testament. How many? (Students repeat the answer.) Ask the following questions. Let students take turns answering. If time permits, ask the questions again without the chart and open Bibles.

What book comes before

Mark? (Matthew)

Romans? (Acts)

Titus? (2 Timothy)

Ephesians? (Galatians)

1 Thessalonians? (Colossians)

Colossians? (Philippians)

John? (Luke)

1 Peter? (James)

What book comes after

Luke? (John)

Hebrews? (James)

Acts? (Romans)

2 John? (3 John)

2 Peter? (1 John)

Philemon? (Hebrews)

Jude? (Revelation)

2 Timothy? (Titus)

Class integration: Library time will help familiarize students with books of the Bible so that finding verses will be easier. Ask the last question about the book from which your lesson is taken.

New Bible Math

Time involved: Five to six minutes

Supplies: A copy of the coded message for each student, pencils

How-to for NEW BIBLE MATH:

Hand out the code, coded message and pencils. Give students about four minutes to decode the message. You will need to help younger students, or do it as a group activity.

Code:

A = 2	B = 4	C = 6	D = 8	E = 10	F = 12	G = 14	H = 16	I = 18	J = 20
K = 22	L = 24	M = 26	N = 1	O = 3	P = 5	Q = 7	R = 9	S = 11	T = 13
U = 15	V = 17	W = 19	X = 21	Y = 23	Z = 25				

Decode this message: 24 3 17 10 10 2 6 16 3 13 16 10 9.

Class integration: Make up a coded message that brings out the point of the lesson. If time permits, students may make up their own lesson-related coded messages for classmates to solve.

Autumn Holiday Ideas

Discoveries

Time involved: Four or five minutes

Supplies: A list of Discoveries activities for each student, Bibles, pencils, stickers

How-to for DISCOVERIES:

Give each student a copy of the Discoveries activity, a Bible, and a pencil. Each discovery is hidden in a Bible verse. Students must find them and write them down. Go over the answers together. Let students check their own answers. Give each a sticker for good work. Read the Bible verses aloud for younger students, and let them give their answers verbally.

Discoveries

1. Discover how Columbus traveled. (2 Chronicles 20:37)
2. Discover what country hired Columbus. (Romans 15:24)
3. Discover what country Columbus came from. (Acts 27:1)
4. Discover where Abraham came from. (Genesis 11:28)
5. Discover Joshua's greatest victory. (Hebrews 11:30)
6. Discover where Joseph was made a slave. (Genesis 39:1)
7. Discover Jonah's mission field. (Jonah 3:2)
8. Discover our final home. (Revelation 11:12)

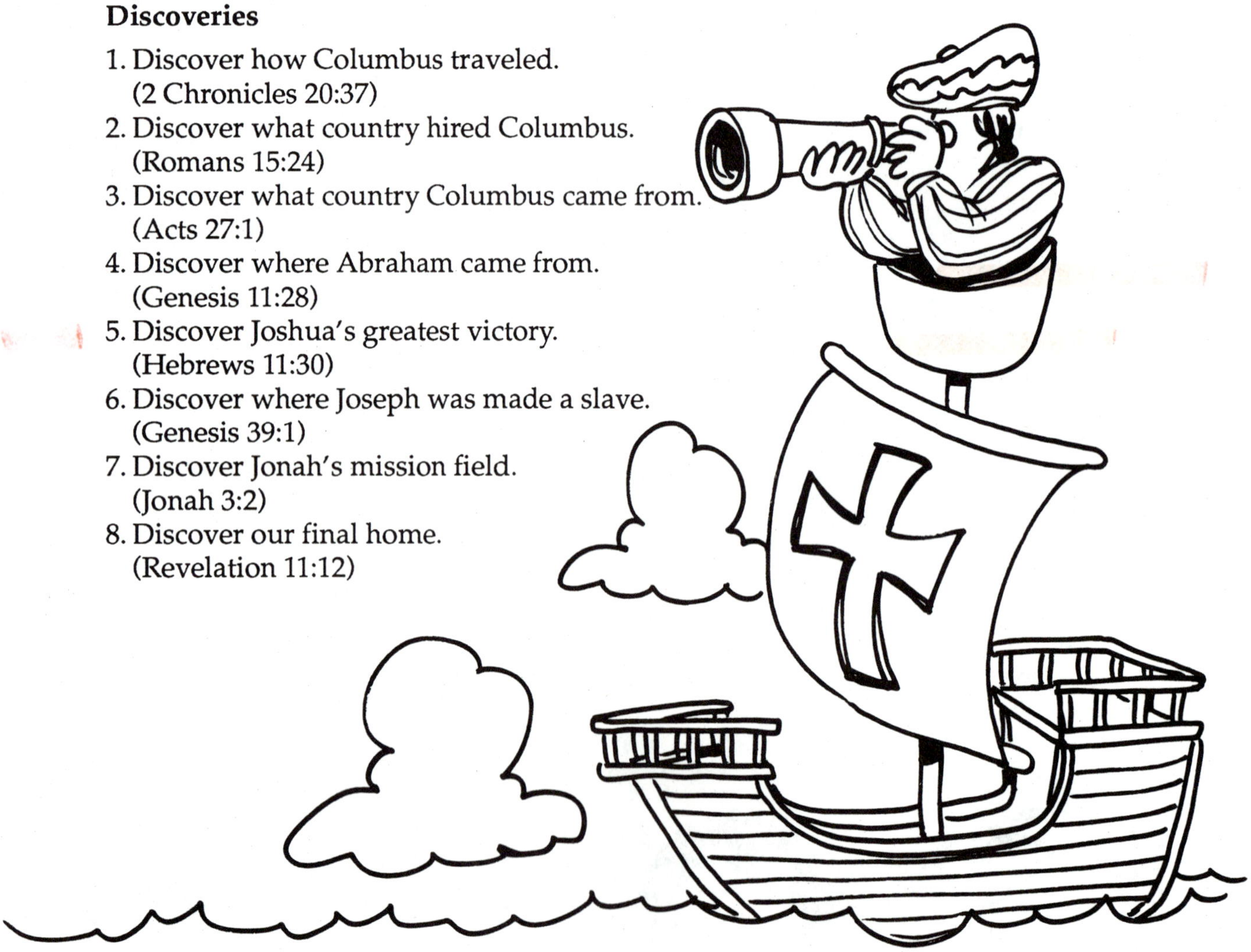

Answers: 1. sailed, 2. Spain, 3. Italy, 4. Ur, 5. Jericho, 6. Egypt, 7. Ninevah, 8. heaven

Class integration: Begin the lesson with this activity. Then tell students that you're going to make some discoveries together in God's Word.

Card-O-Gram

Time involved: Four to five minutes

Supplies: Light-colored construction paper or typing paper, colored markers

How-to for CARD-O-GRAM:

Ask students why we celebrate Columbus Day. (It's the birthday of the man who discovered America.) Explain that the most important discovery we can make is Jesus Christ. Let the class make cards for friends or relatives, telling about their discovery of Jesus. Hand out paper which students may fold in half. Print this card suggestion on the board for students who need help: (Front) Wishing you a happy Columbus Day! (Inside) I've made a discovery too–new life in Jesus! Suggest Bible verses which students may use: John 1:12, Acts 16:31. Encourage each child to give the card to someone.

Class integration: Use this opportunity to check with each student about her faith. Invite those who have not yet accepted Jesus to do so today. Those who have accepted Jesus may reword their cards to tell others how to discover Jesus.

Columbus Spell

Time involved: Five minutes

How-to for COLUMBUS SPELL:

Seat students in a circle. Have them hold out their hands, palms up. Go around the circle, clapping each student's hands with yours, spelling out C-O-L-U-M-B-U-S, one letter per child. The student you say "s" to stands and says a favorite Bible verse. Sit in his chair and let that student be "it." "It" goes around the room, spelling C-O-L-U-M-B-U-S and clapping hands. The next "s" student stands, says another verse, and becomes "it." Continue until everyone has said at least one verse.

Class integration: Use this activity as a fun break in the lesson. It may encourage students to memorize Scripture.

If I Could Be Columbus

Time involved: Five minutes

How-to for IF I COULD BE COLUMBUS:

Write on the chalkboard, "If I could be Columbus, I would discover. . . ." Ask students to complete the sentence, adding what they think would make life better. Example: "If I could be Columbus, I would discover a way to do my homework at the push of a button." After the fun ideas, go around again and have the class think of spiritual discoveries. Example: "If I could be Columbus, I would discover how to remember to pray before I get myself into trouble." Let each student give a suggestion.

Class integration: Discuss the idea that discoveries don't always come easily; we have to work at them. As we study the Bible and pray, God helps us discover new things about Him and about life.

Changing Prayer Requests

Time involved: Three to five minutes

Supplies: Small slips of paper, pencils

How-to for CHANGING PRAYER REQUESTS:

The seasons change, and so do we. Discuss what kinds of changes students feel they need to make their lives more pleasing to God. Hand out paper and pencils and ask students to write prayer requests to give you. Promise to pray for them. Promise them also not to make their requests public. Younger students may share their prayer requests verbally, instead of writing them.

LORD, I NEED YOU TO HELP ME TO BE MORE PATIENT.

Class integration: Use this as a time to get to know your students. Share prayer requests of your own and ask the class to pray about them. Use this activity at the end of the lesson.

Letter Changes

Time involved: Four to five minutes

Supplies: A copy of Letter Changes for each student, pencils

How-to for LETTER CHANGES:

Give each student a copy of Letter Changes. Talk about how fall brings many changes: cooler weather, beautifully colored leaves, and busy schedules at school and church. Have students change one letter in each "word" on the list, and they will find something God wants them to do or be in the fall and in every season. Then ask students to share the "changes" they made.

1. S -T-U-B-Y (study)
2. O-B-E-T (obey)
3. P-R-E-Y (pray)
4. D-I-N-G (sing)
5. B-E-A-D (read)
6. H-E-L-D (help)
7. S-H-A-D-E (share)
8. N-O (go)
9. J-E-M-O-R-I-Z-E (memorize)
10. F-R-I-T-H-F-U-L (faithful)

I'M GOING TO BEGIN TO MEMORIZE THE WORD.
AND I'M GOING TO START BEING MORE FAITHFUL.

Class integration: Many things get in the way of what God wants us to do. But daily prayer, Bible reading, and a desire to please the Lord will help us change. Lead students in prayer before class is dismissed. Ask God to help them make the changes in their lives that He wants.

Leaf Changes

Time involved: Four to five minutes

Supplies: Several large, colored fall leaves, black markers, clear Con-Tact paper, scissors

How-to for LEAF CHANGES:

Ask students what they like about the fall season. Let each choose a fall leaf on which to print the memory verse with a marker. Then give each one a piece of clear Con-Tact paper. The student should encase the leaf in the Con-Tact; then cut it out to preserve the leaf verse.

HE IS LIKE A TREE PLANTED BY STREAMS OF WATER, WHICH YIELDS ITS FRUIT IN SEASON AND WHOSE LEAF DOES NOT WITHER. WHATEVER HE DOES PROSPERS.
(PSALM 1:3)

Class integration: Use today's memory verse for this activity. Encourage students to take their leaves home and memorize the verse.

Opposite Changes

Time involved: Four or five minutes

Supplies: NIV Bibles

How-to for OPPOSITE CHANGES:

Read Galatians 5:22-23 to the class. Hand out the Opposite Changes list and have students match each wrong attitude or action with the opposite fruit of the Spirit. Set the timer for three minutes. When time is up, go over the answers together.

Opposite Changes

1. hate	kindness
2. sadness	love
3. fighting	self-control
4. too anxious	patience
5. mean to people	joy
6. refuse to help	gentleness
7. undependable	goodness
8. tough	faithfulness
9. temper tantrum	peace

Answers: 1. love, 2. joy, 3. peace, 4. patience, 5. kindness, 6. goodness, 7. faithfulness, 8. gentleness, 9. self-control

Class integration: A change in seasons can be a good time for change in our lives. Use this activity at the end of the class. Pray with students for effective change, starting now.

Holiday Spinner

Time involved: Four to five minutes

Supplies: A game spinner made from a cardboard circle, a thumbtack, a paper clip

How-to for HOLIDAY SPINNER:

Before class, make a game spinner. Cut out a large cardboard circle. Divide it into six equal sections. Print one of the holidays listed below on each section of the circle. Thumbtack a paper clip to the center for a spinner. Each student will spin to determine what holiday his question will be about. If the spinner lands on Veterans Day, the student gets two turns. Each correct answer gives the student 1000 points. No answer may be given twice. Once an answer has been used, the next student must think of a different answer to the question.

Veterans Day: What is a war in which the United States has fought?

Labor Day: What is a type of labor or work we can do for the Lord?

Memorial Day: Name a person in the Bible. How did that person die?

New Year's Day: What is a resolution that would be good to follow this year?

April Fools' Day: Who was a Bible person who acted like a fool?

Flag Day: Name a Bible place. What happened there?

Class integration: Make up your own game questions to apply to the day's lesson. Use this game as an introduction to the lesson or as a review.

Make Me a Veteran

Time involved: Three to five minutes

How-to for MAKE ME A VETERAN:

Veterans are soldiers who have come home after battle. We can be God's veterans when we don't give in to Satan or yield to his temptation. Share a personal testimony of a victory over temptation. Ask students to share some of their victories or defeats. Encourage children by reminding them that they are becoming veterans in God's service.

Class integration: Use this activity at the close of the lesson. Discuss confession, forgiveness and victory. Then pray for God's help in resisting temptation.

Lineups

Time involved: Four to five minutes

Supplies: A copy of the Lineups game for each student, pencils

How-to for LINEUPS:

Give each student a copy of Lineups and a pencil. Allow students three minutes to draw lines from the wars to their beginning dates. Go over the answers together. Explain that those who know Jesus are always ready for spiritual battle. With younger students, you may prefer to just discuss wars and why they happen.

Lineups

1. World War I	1957
2. War of 1812	1917
3. Revolutionary War	1950
4. Civil War	1941
5. Korean War	1991
6. Desert Storm	1775
7. Vietnam War	1860
8. World War II	1812

YOU MEAN THE WAR OF 1812 WASN'T IN 1775?

Answers: 1. 1917, 2. 1812, 3. 1775, 4. 1860, 5. 1950, 6. 1991, 7. 1957, 8. 1941

Class integration: We all want peace, but in this world there will always be war until Jesus comes again. Explain that we don't have to be afraid of war when we trust God, because He has promised to watch over us and help us.

Insignias

Time involved: Five minutes

Supplies: Insignias of U.S. Army, Air Force, Navy, Marines, Coast Guard and/or Canadian Armed Forces; construction paper; glue; scissors; colored markers

How-to for INSIGNIAS:

Show the armed forces' insignias. Let students look at them carefully. Ask if they know people who served in the armed forces. Let each student draw an insignia for a branch of the service, and glue it on a piece of construction paper. Under the insignia, the student may print "Praise the Lord, All You Nations." Psalm 117:1a

PRAISE
THE LORD,
ALL YOU
NATIONS

Class integration: Veterans Day is a time to remember people who have died to keep our freedom. Jesus died so we could have freedom from sin. End class with this activity and a time of silently praising God.

Thanks or Grumbles

Time involved: Five minutes

How-to for THANKS OR GRUMBLES:

Seat the class in a circle. Go around the circle, pointing to students one at a time. The first one you point to is "Thanks," the second is "Grumbles." Continue around the circle this way; then stop at a student. If that student is "Thanks," he must tell what he is thankful for. If he is "Grumbles," the student must tell something he grumbles about. That student becomes "it," and goes around the room as you did, stopping at a student of his choice. Continue until everyone has been "it."

Class integration: End class with this activity. Emphasize that we all should be thankful. Have a time of prayer, confessing the sin of grumbling. Thank God for what He has done for us.

11/7/93

Turkey Feathers

Time involved: Four to five minutes

Supplies: A picture of a turkey, two paper outlines of feathers for each student, colored markers or crayons, cellophane tape

How-to for TURKEY FEATHERS:

Hold up the picture of the turkey. Hand out the paper feathers and markers or crayons. Ask each student to decorate two feathers for the turkey. Have students write a thank-you to God on each feather; then cut them out. Let students come up one by one, share their thank-yous, and tape their feathers to the turkey's tail.

Class integration: Thanksgiving is a good time to thank God for His blessings and to thank people for what they've done for us. Use this activity for a break in the lesson or as a time of praise at the end of the lesson.

Find and Learn

Time involved: Three to five minutes

Supplies: A Bible for each student

How-to for FIND AND LEARN:

Have each student find a Bible verse that expresses praise or thanks to God. After showing the verse to you, the student should memorize it. Psalm 150:6, Psalm 100:4, and Philippians 4:6 are good praise verses to memorize. After a few minutes, ask students to recite their verses. With younger children, choose a praise verse to memorize as a group.

LET EVERYTHING
THAT HAS BREATH
PRAISE THE
LORD.

Class integration: End the lesson with this activity. Pray that students will be thankful every day. Make sure they understand the words they memorize. Ask them to say their verses to you as they leave the room.

Roundtable Talk

Time involved: Five minutes

How-to for ROUNDTABLE TALK:

Talk about the importance of expressing our thanks to people and to God. Go around the table, asking students to say why they are thankful for specific people in their lives. Then have each student give thanks to God for some blessing.

Class integration: Conclude the lesson with a prayer of thanksgiving for the Bible and for the privilege of studying it together. Remind students that it is through the Bible that we learn to give thanks and praise to God.

Dinner Hunt

Time involved: Five minutes

Supplies: Pens or pencils, paper, copied list of verses, Bibles

How-to for DINNER HUNT:

Give each student a Bible verse list, a Bible, and a pencil. Have the class look up the verses to decide the menu for their Thanksgiving dinner. After four minutes, have students put down their pencils and share their answers. Award 1000 points for each correct answer. Give a round of applause for each student with at least 5000 points. With younger students, read the verses aloud and let them listen for the foods you mention.

Verses	Answers
1. Matthew 23:37	hen or chicken
2. Daniel 1:12	vegetables
3. Matthew 4:4	bread
4. Deuteronomy 32:10	apple
5. Exodus 3:8	milk, honey
6. 2 Samuel 6:19	dates and raisins
7. Exodus 29:23	cake
8. Psalm 63:5	richest of foods

Class integration: Use this activity for a fun break in the lesson. Encourage students to make Thanksgiving not just a day of eating too much, but a day of thanking God.

Christmas Cover-Ups

Time involved: Five to seven minutes

Supplies: A sheet of 12" x 18" drawing paper for each child, assorted colored markers or crayons, stapler

How-to for CHRISTMAS COVER-UPS:

Hand out paper and markers. Print on the chalkboard the list of Christmas scenes found below. Have each student choose one to illustrate. He should leave a 1" margin on the right so that words from John 3:16 can be added.

- the angel speaking to Mary
- the stable
- the shepherds in the field
- the star
- the Magi find Jesus
- the dream of Joseph
- the baby in the manger
- the shepherds find Jesus
- the Magi inquire about Jesus

When the pictures are completed, staple them together in order. Print a phrase from John 3:16 on the right margin of each page. Design an attractive cover for the Christmas book and share it with the class.

Class integration: Use a Christmas verse that correlates with the aim of your lesson. Encourage students to make their own Christmas books at home to share with family and friends.

Card-O-Grams

Time involved: Five minutes

Supplies: Construction paper, scissors, glue, markers, Christmas stickers, pictures from recycled cards

How-to for CARD-O-GRAMS:

Talk about people who don't have family and friends and may be lonely at Christmas. If possible, contact a nearby nursing home and arrange to "adopt" a lonely person. Hand out construction paper and other art supplies. Have students make Christmas cards for their special persons or for other lonely people they know. Discuss a Bible verse to include on the cards. Students may sign their cards and leave them with you to deliver.

Class integration: God gave His Son for us. We should give of ourselves to others because we know and love Jesus. Use this activity at the end of the lesson. Encourage students to include in their cards a message from the day's lesson. If possible, take your class to personally deliver their cards.

Trim a Tree

Time involved: Four to five minutes

Supplies: A 12" green construction paper Christmas tree and a cardboard stand for each student, scissors, gummed stars, colored markers, glue

How-to for TRIM A TREE:

Give each student a Christmas tree to cut out. Choose two or three Bible verses from the lesson to write on the trees. Students may write the verses on ornament shapes or in the shape of garland strung around the trees. Have each student choose a verse to memorize. After he recites the verse correctly, provide the student with stars to add to his tree. Keep the trees in the classroom until shortly before Christmas. Then let students take them home.

Bible verses:

John 3:16
Luke 2:14
Matthew 1:21
Matthew 2:10
Luke 2:11
Isaiah 9:6

Class integration: Use this fun activity to help students learn Bible verses important to the day's lesson.

Musical Gifts

Time involved: Five minutes

Supplies: Six small gift-wrapped boxes containing instructions (from the list below)

How-to for MUSICAL GIFTS:

Seat the class in a circle. Have students pass a gift around the circle as music is played. When the music stops, the one holding it must open it and do what the card inside says. That student then starts passing around another gift box as the music plays again. Continue until all six gifts have been used.

Gift instructions:

1. Quote a Christmas Bible verse.
2. Tell the story of the shepherds.
3. Name the three gifts the Magi brought to Jesus.
4. Tell the class about a gift we could give to help someone learn about Jesus.
5. Sing (or quote the words to) a Christmas carol.
6. Give a quiz to the class.
   a. Who told Mary about her baby? (angel)
   b. Where was Jesus born? (Bethlehem)
   c. In what book of the Bible do we find the story of the Magi? (Matthew)
   d. Who ordered the census? (Caesar)
   e. Where was Mary when the angel spoke to her? (Nazareth)
   f. Who was engaged to Mary? (Joseph)
   g. Who told the shepherds that the Savior was born? (angel)
   h. Where did Mary and Joseph take Jesus to escape Herod? (Egypt)

Class integration: Use this fun activity to teach the lesson. Include the Christmas Bible story, memory verse, etc., in the gift boxes.

Add-On Greeting

Time involved: Five minutes

How-to for ADD-ON GREETING:

Seat students in a circle. Together, they will say a Christmas greeting, one word per student. The first greeting may be humorous, such as "Have a merry, happy, jolly, ho-ho-ho Christmas!" The second time around, the greeting should express the true meaning of Christmas, such as "I wish you a peaceful Christmas because of the Prince of Peace." Each student must remember all the previous words; then add one more until the greeting is completed.

Class integration: Students are excited at Christmastime. This activity may be used as a break in the lesson to let them have some fun and to remind them of the seriousness of the holiday. It will also help them think of ways they can be testimonies to friends and relatives.

Vowel Detective

Time involved: Five minutes

Supplies: A copy of the Vowel Detective verse for each student, pencils

How-to for VOWEL DECTECTIVE:

Hand out the verse and pencils. Give students three minutes to add the missing vowels to the verse. Then have them read the verse in unison. Work together for a couple of minutes to memorize the verse.

Gl_ry t_ G_d _n th_ h_gh_st,

_nd _n _ _rth p_ _c_ t_ m_n

_n wh_m h_s f_v_r r_sts.

Luke 2:14

Class integration: Choose a verse important to the lesson, to fit this activity in with your aim. Suggest that students choose other verses and play this game at home with their families.